In the Waiting Time © 2020 Emily R. Long

Printed in the United States of America
First Printing 2020

ISBN: 978-1-7356281-0-3

Library of Congress Control Number: 2020917989

Firefly Grace Publishing
Burlington, VT 05403
www.EmilyRLong.com

Cover Image: Wolfgang Hasselman (Unsplash)

In the Waiting Time

Messages from Infertility Warriors

Gratitude

For all those who have been, or still remain, in the waiting time.

Other Available Books by Emily Long

Invisible Mothers: When Love Doesn't Die

You Are Not Alone: Love Letters from Loss Mom to Loss Mom

From Father to Father: Letters from Loss Dad to Loss Dad

Life Without the Baby Journal: Redefining Life, Motherhood and Self After Loss

From Mother to Mother: On the Loss of a Child

Fathers Speak: On the Death of a Child

Pregnancy After Loss Support: Love Letters from Loss Mom to Loss Mom (with Lindsey Henke)

Index of Letters

*** Latinx
^ No living children and no longer trying
~ Queer
"" Use of Surrogate
* Wife and Husband
++ Religious/Spiritual
Single
^ ^ ^ Disabled
$ Hysterectomy

FOREWARD

When you've been diagnosed with infertility, the uncertainty of the journey ahead leaves you vulnerable. You want to be understood, heard, and seen. Instead, we become lost and entangled in the deepest recesses of our minds. Add the constant perfection portrayed on social media and your left feeling like there's no room for the sometimes ugly parts of infertility and recurrent loss. It's no wonder that a large percentage of the 1 in 8 couples who suffer from infertility remain silent.

While it is evident that the contributing writers come from various backgrounds, the shared theme of community and support reminds the reader that they are not alone. Infertility often makes one feel like a failure, eating away at your self-esteem. You can be a CEO, delivery-driver, Doctor, or part of the LGBTQ community, infertility does not discriminate.

You will learn to be honest with yourself and by doing so, discover that honesty with loved ones becomes easier. Expecting friends and family who have never lived through this to understand is unfair, which is why this book is indispensable. You may not be able to control your diagnosis, but you can control what and with whom you share this intimate part of your life. Be intentional about your mental and emotional health along your journey; healing is attainable while in the midst.

Monique Farook
September 13, 2020

Creator and Host of *Infertility and Me Podcast*
www.infertilityandmepodcast.com
IG: @infertilityandmepodcast

Letters

In the Waiting. . .

The clinical definition of infertility is the inability
to become pregnant after at least a year of trying to
conceive. The other most common definition refers to
secondary infertility, those who have been able to get
pregnant one or more times, but are now unable to
become pregnant.

In this book, I also define infertility as the inability to
carry a pregnancy to term and suffering miscarriage or
stillbirth, including recurrent pregnancy loss with no
living child. As many know, too often it's some painful
combination of these definitions.

I personally have never known the struggle to get
pregnant, for me that came all to easily, but I do know
the pain of never being able to carry a baby to a living birth and repeatedly having my babies die in my
womb.

I want to make note and acknowledge here that not
all who seek fertility treatment struggle with infertility,
as many LGBTQ+ or single parent families can attest.
However, infertility does strikes hard and painfully at
families of every demographic - no one is immune.

Some families, however, struggle with even less support and a decreased quality care than others. Our
friends living in marginalized bodies are often navigating not just infertility but also biased medical
care, stigma and harmful stereotypes, reduced access
to resources and support options, and fewer visible
examples of experiences from people like them. This

is long overdue to change. I believe one small way to help create that change is by making space for everyone's story to be told AND by listening to the stories of others.

I truly believe that everyone deserves to see themselves in the story of someone like them. My hope is that in the pages of this book, you find someone that resonates, words and experiences you connect with, and stories that make you feel less alone. It is perhaps an impossible task, but one I will never stop striving to accomplish.

I believe in the power of stories. I believe in their power to heal, to connect us, to guide us, to share history and inspire courage, to teach and empower. More than a therapist, more than merely a writer, above all I consider myself a storyteller and a story witness. It is an honor and a privilege.

Infertility does not always have a happy ending, at least, not that one we expect. Often, yes we are able to add to our family as hoped, but always, no. I myself do not and will not have any living children. Fortunately, this does not mean I am without hope.

I don't believe that hope comes from blind promises of happy endings. That is a false hope too frequently harming rather than helping. I'm not even sure it comes from the expected happy endings themselves.

True hope comes from acknowledging the messiness of life - the uncertainty, the uncomfortable, the shrouded path ahead. To acknowledge the hard truths and take the next step anyway. To keep moving, growing, learning, fighting - LIVING - no matter what the outcome or the obstacles on the journey.

Hope comes from knowing that no matter how uncertain or messy life may be, others are with us through every up and down. WE, our connection to each other, are the hope that finds the light in the dark.

I cannot guarantee that you'll be able to add to your family as you wish to, but I promise say that you aren't alone.

When things feel dark and hopeless, let us – through these words and stories shared in love - be your beacon. Let us carry your hope.

With all my love and hope,

Emily

True hope comes from acknowledging the messiness of life - the uncertainty, the uncomfortable, the shrouded path ahead. To acknowledge the hard truths and take the next step anyway. To keep moving, growing, learning, fighting - LIVING - no matter what the outcome or the obstacles on the journey.

Amy

Dear One Struggling to Conceive,

I am so sorry you are going through this.

I'm so sorry you have to sit and wait while EVERY-BODY else is announcing their pregnancies.

I'm sorry that you are forced to seek medical intervention and pay money to have a child while the rest of the world gets to have babies for free.

I'm sorry that the people around you don't understand the monthly roller coaster ride you are on.

I am sorry that they don't understand the hormonal changes your body is going through on fertility medication.

I'm sorry for it all.

After a year of trying with no success, we were forced to seek medical intervention. Making that initial appointment was devastating to me. It felt like we were giving up, like we weren't able to do something everyone else could. When I shared this fear with my friends, I was told to "just relax," "you are overthinking it," or "trying is the fun part." (It took all my might not to punch those people in the face when they said those things.)

All responses from people who had no idea the monthly roller coaster rides I had experienced for an entire year. All from people who never struggled to conceive. It made me feel completely alone in my pain and frustration.

We started off slow, dipping our toe into the fertility pond by taking Clomid (the fertility gateway drug) and doing timed intercourse. Over the course of 5 months, we progressed to Clomid and IUI; Clomid, trigger shots, and IUI; and finally ending with Clomid, injectables, and IUI. That cycle was the one to give us our first ever positive pregnancy test. Unfortunately, that pregnancy ended in a missed miscarriage and more heartache.

After one natural pregnancy, conceived after our miscarriage, which ended with our son being stillborn, we eventually returned to fertility treatments. This time we brought in the big guns, the last step before heading to IVF for us, and did strictly injectable cycles. These cycles involved daily injections, every other day blood draws, ultrasound appointments, suppression shots, trigger shots, and progesterone suppositories (FUN!).

After two cycles of this protocol, we conceived twin girls who were born healthy and happy in August of 2018.

I share all this, not to scare you, but tell you that you are not alone. There are so many of us who have struggled and who understand your pain.

My biggest saving grace was reconnecting with an old friend, who was in the midst of IVF, when I confided to her about our struggle. From that moment on, we talked daily and she became my infertility guru. She listened when I shared of yet another negative test. She talked me down when I was on an emotional ledge. She understood the unnecessary bitterness I felt towards friends and family who were having babies so easily.

Find your infertile friend. Find that person you can go to when you need to share the dark emotions that inevitably come along with struggling to conceive. Find the person who confirms that you are not alone in this. They can be "in real life" friends or "virtual" friends, anyone who makes you feel understood.

You are not the only person who has been dealt this crappy hand, and unfortunately, you won't be the last. There are plenty of us out there who are willing to walk through it with you. While sitting in the wait, let us sit with you, hold your hand, and commiserate over how much this sucks.

Sending all the baby dust your way,

Amy Lied

Doggiebagsnotdiaperbags.wordpress.com

Find your infertile friend. Find that person you can go to when you need to share the dark emotions that inevitably come along with struggling to conceive. Find the person who confirms that you are not alone in this. They can be "in real life" friends or "virtual" friends, anyone who makes you feel understood.

Rocío

Hola[1],

First things first, tu no está sola[2]. This journey is one of the most difficult paths you will be taking mentally, physically, and spiritually. Pero[3] like I said before, Tú no estás sola!

Looking around sometimes in our community you might think that you are not living in your fullest potential of your "Latinidad." From not being fertile, to not depicting what is consistently portrayed on television; especially when you are watching your telenovelas[4], is hard. Pero, tú no estás sola.

Going through this infertility journey, I remember feeling as if a tornado was coming in my direction and being convinced it wasn't going to hit me, as it was hitting me. To have the conversation with my husband, and look him in the eyes and tell him, "Hi, your wife is defective, so…want to grab a drink and a hookah?" I tried my best to block the option of going through fertility treatment out of my mind because obviously they (the doctors) are wrong. I also had to prepare myself for my Latinx community giving me giving me unsolicited advice on how to get pregnant. Telling me tips and tricks that their forefathers forefathers told them like:

---

1   Hi
2   You are not alone
3   But
4   Latin soap opera

"La próxima vez levanta tus piernas sobre tu cabeza y espera 15 minutos"[5]

"Tomate un jarabe! La hija de la vecina hizo eso y salió embarazada"[6]

"Llega a la casa borracha porque así sale uno embarazado más rápido"[7]

"Rebaja, que la gordura no ayuda"[8]
"Tienes que tener más fe"[9]

You are now placed into a situation where you are the teacher and the student. It Sucks. You are educating yourself, your significant other, your family and friends. People will start saying all of the above and even mas[10]. You are going to get touched by strangers. Probed, fondled, examined and all while going through this psychological mess in your head. Pero, tú no estás sola!

You have apoyo! You have support! In these pages, you are surrounded by women who have crossed the oceans and borders for liberty. You come from a line of women who have had to make a way out of no way. It's ok to cry, it's ok to feel down, it's ok to feel. Some-times it's better to kick rocks on your journey than kick

5   Next time raise your legs over your head and wait 15 minutes
6   Drink a remedy! The neighbor's daughter did and she ended up pregnant.
7   Get drunk, that's the quickest way to end up pregnant.
8   Lose weight, being fat doesn't help.
9   You need to have more faith
10   More

air and be still.

Here is some advice from me, an Afro-Latina that sees life through very comical eyes so prepárate[11]!

1. Get used to the feel of a one-night stand! Because people you don't know, who you just met will know your insides better than you will! Their names, not important, all you know is that you are there, spread eagle, hoping and praying everything looks ok to move on to the next thing.
2. Doctors are never close to your vagina; they are always closer to your feet. Keep them clean. Take a pair of medias[12] with you.
3. Always take a bag with you. They do not have a cubby to place your underwear, shoes or pants. It's a chair. You don't want your panties tucked away in your pants and then you can't find them when the doctor leaves and you have to get dressed, and then when you turn your pants inside out for the thousandth time they fall gently on the floor. You will be pissed and even madder when you have to put them on. Take a bag and an extra pair of socks, thank me later.
4. Always remember, the goal is to become a parent, not just to go through fertility drugs. There are different paths to become a parent. Fertility drugs are just one path.
5. La gente hablaran mierda[13]. Ignore them.
6. Tu familia hablaran mierda[14]. Ignore them.
7. This journey belongs to you and your partner.
8. You deserve your alone time. Para que nadiete-

---

11   Prepare yourself
12   Socks
13   People will talk shit
14   Your family will talk shit

jodas.[15]

9. Don't apologize for your emotions, let them out at all costs
10. This is your partner's journey también.[16]
11. It's ok not to go to your second cousin's best friend's baby shower. They'll live.
12. Always make sure to do things that bring you joy.
13. Distractions are an awesome mental vacation, but don't stay there.
14. Remember any step forward, no matter how small, is still a step forward. Recuerde que cualquier paso adelante, por pequeño que sea, sigue siendo un paso adelante.

Rocio Beauvais

Host and creator of:
Tootsie Rolaids Life's Sweet Relief Podcast

---

15   So no one bothers you
16   Also

Looking around sometimes in our community you might think that you are not living in your fullest potential of your "Latinidad." From not being fertile, to not depicting what is consistently portrayed on television; especially when you are watching your telenovelas[17], is hard. Pero, tú no estás sola.

Jenna

To my heartbroken friend,

Let me begin by telling you how sorry I am that you are experiencing infertility. I'm sorry you are hurting. I wish I could tell you some magic words to make all of this stop happening and to heal your hurting heart. But I can't. After everything I've been through, I still don't have the answers. Infertility is so hard and complicated. Instead, I will share some of my experience in the hopes that it will help you to feel less alone. I'm also writing in an attempt to give you hope that you will get through this, one day at time.

My infertility is a story of half agony, half hope. The agony was heavy, horrible, and heartbreaking. Hope was so hard to find at times that I wasn't sure there was any left, but I knew I needed it to keep going. For so long I felt lost in a dark place with my heart broken, trying to collect all of the pieces and put them back together; trying to make sense of the mess around me and the uncertainty of my future; trying to keep functioning, despite feeling so broken, angry, and alone.

The grief I experienced during my years of infertility was overwhelming. Each and every cycle of failure was heartbreaking, and the accumulation of losses felt nearly unbearable. I grieved the loss of so many hopes and dreams; the loss of what I expected life to be like;

the loss of my first pregnancy which was ectopic; the loss of friends who did not stand by me; the losses of time, energy, and money. My infertility was profound grief on so many levels.

I had some really, really hard days. At times I failed to see the point of my life at all. I didn't want to move or get dressed. I didn't want to visit with friends. When I was drowning in grief, I simply had nothing to say and making small talk was unbearable. In between episodes of intense grief, I felt numb. I would go through the motions of my day, without real awareness or any enthusiasm I might normally have. I would try to be "normal" at work, try to smile or make jokes... then I'd return home and stare at the wall. I felt like I was living a lie, like no one could actually see me and the pain I was in.

It's almost easy to forget how hard bad days can be once they are over... I had a lot of ups and downs during infertility, and each time I found myself having really, really hard days again I was amazed that I had even made it through days like that before. I looked back at previous dark days and I wondered how the hell I got through them.

The only answer I can come up with is: one day at a time.

I don't know the secret to getting through bad days.

I don't know the secret to fixing a broken heart or surviving grief. But I know that all of these are experiences I had to work through. There's no detour for getting around this kind of agony. There are things I did to help myself along the way, but in the end, the only way out of a hard experience is through it -- one hard day at a time.

So one day at a time, I tried to take care of myself. I let myself feel sad. I sat around and cried. A lot. I turned down social invitations and ignored phone calls. I spent hours reading about infertility, about grief, about hope. I went to a support group, where I met and spent time with friends who understood what I was going through. I wrote in my journal. I blogged. My husband did his best to support me, and I was so lost in my own grief that I rarely even thought to ask how I might help him. Grief sometimes looks selfish, but it's not. Grieving is hard, personal work and it must be done to find healing.

And one day at a time, I looked for hope. Everywhere. I learned to redefine what hope looked like when all hope was lost: What can I hope for now? I needed hope that my life would be beautiful again, that I wouldn't always be living in the agony of infertility. And while we kept hoping for a living child, we were faced with the possibility of life without one, so we kept hoping that we'd be able to find peace with wherever life took us. I celebrated small things, everyday

things. I went on walks and practiced yoga. I ate choc-
olate and drank champagne. I watched my favorite TV
shows and colored intricate designs. I planted flowers
and trees. I practiced gratitude. I looked for rainbows,
for all of the good things in my life, the lights shining
in the darkness: friends, experiences, moments.

Writing everything down like this makes it sound like
I did a great job taking care of myself and navigating my grief, but that's certainly not how it felt in the
moment. It felt horrible and like it was never going to
end. Trying to grow my family was the hardest thing
I have ever done. I remember telling my mom that
I wished I could just be sedated until it was all over,
but that wasn't an option. So I did what I had to do to
continue on and get through each day.

I don't know what you'll need to do to get through
your days while you wait, grieve, and hope; while
you face hard decisions and an uncertain future. My
hope for you is that you will be gentle with yourself
and take care of yourself, one day at a time. Time is
healing, and while infertility may always hurt some, it
won't always be this agonizing. No one knows how or
when your infertility will be resolved, but you won't
always be in this dark painful place. In some way you
will be able to move forward in a direction and things
will get better. By taking care of yourself in many
small ways, you'll be able to get through this one day
at a time.

It's hard to be stuck in a place of half agony and half hope, and I know you might feel alone in the darkness -- I often did -- but there are others traveling alongside you right now, and there are those of us who have been there before. You are not alone. I see you. I feel your heartache, and I mourn with you.

I'm holding light and hope for you, sending my love, and wishing you peace.

Jenna

www.iamhalfhope.com

I don't know the secret to getting through bad days. I don't know the secret to fixing a broken heart or surviving grief. But I know that all of these are experiences I had to work through. There's no detour for getting around this kind of agony. There are things I did to help myself along the way, but in the end, the only way out of a hard experience is through it -- one hard day at a time.

Amy

Dear Reader,

When I started my fertility journey, I was not very optimistic I was 40, and I knew that time wasn't on my side. I didn't know if it was even still possible to have a healthy pregnancy and a living baby. I knew the medical data and the odds, and I know many tragic case studies: friends who had lost their pregnancies or their children. I was awash in doubts about being a single mom, starting so late in life, bringing a child into the world as it is right now, the cost of fertility treatments, and how small the chance was that I could conceive at all. My head was full, and left little room for me to listen to my heart.

I started fertility treatments on my own, after about six months of research, listening to an amazing fertility podcast (Spermcast, hosted by Molly Hawkey), searching sperm donor websites, and talking to all of my friends and family – and some strangers too.

Against all the odds, I was pregnant after my first IUI (intrauterine insemination, performed by a nurse named Kathy, with donor sperm from a stranger known only as "Plato"). Seeing the positive pregnancy test cracked open my heart, I was elated. I had tried so hard to keep hope at bay, for fear of the crushing disappointment if things didn't work out.

I started to have symptoms: tender, painful breasts, exhaustion, and an upset tummy. I went to my six week ultrasound...and I saw my baby! I saw her heartbeat, fluttering away at a strong 118 beats per minute. And that's when my heart opened up the rest of the way. I can't describe the magic of seeing my baby; for me, it all became real in that moment, in a way I couldn't have imagined when I walked into the exam room.

And then, all of a sudden, the tone in the room shifted. I could feel a sudden tension, even though the ultrasound technician was silent. When she did speak, she told me that the baby was smaller than it should be at six weeks, and I needed to come back at eight weeks to see if there was any growth.

I conceived on March 17, 2020, just before the coronavirus pandemic shut the world down. The two weeks between ultrasounds were spent at home, alone, just me and my baby. During that time, my pregnancy symptoms waned and disappeared, and I just knew. . .we were parting ways. I was grief stricken. I had tried to steel myself against the pain of this loss with facts and figures, but the pregnancy changed me. My heart was speaking to me now and my heart had fallen in love with my baby.

It's been four months since I conceived her and I am crying as I reflect on my baby, my pregnancy, the loss, and our short time together. But I've found myself changing yet again, I've started feeling really grateful. I am so thankful for her; she came into my life, into my body, into the world, and tried the best she could. We didn't get to be together for very long, but she made me a mother. I was thankful that I had so much time to myself during quarantine – I had the chance to sit with her and savor the feeling of being pregnant. And when I lost her, I could give myself time to cry, to write in my journal, to sit and experience my feelings and think my thoughts. I am grateful to those parents who shared their stories of heartbreak, the ones who taught me how important it is to take every day as it comes and to enjoy a relationship with the baby, no matter how much time you have.

On the day before my last ultrasound – the eight week one when they told me what I already knew in my body – I was sitting outside and I saw a cardinal fly across the yard. Before this experience, I would never have entertained a "spiritual" thought like this one, but on that last day, I felt sure that the cardinal was sent by her spirit to say goodbye. I like the part of me that can embrace a thought like that. And I have my daughter to thank for helping me to feel the world in that way.

If I were to write a letter to myself, and send it back in time before I started on my fertility journey, I would tell myself these things:

- Listen to your heart.
- Trust in the knowledge that you are doing everything in the best way that you can.
- Savor every hopeful, beautiful moment that you pass through.
- Know that you are part of a parenthood stretching out across the world, and across all time. We hold each other tight and hold each other up during our journeys.
- You are not alone.

With love,

Amy Altadonna

Listen to your heart.
Trust in the knowledge that you are doing everything in the best way that you can.
Savor every hopeful, beautiful moment that you pass through.
Know that you are part of a parenthood stretching out across the world, and across all time. We hold each other tight and hold each other up during our journeys.
You are not alone.

Desiree

Dear Warriors,

I want to share my story, especially with those that are single, in abusive relationships, disabled or have had second trimester miscarriages.

My two second trimester miscarriages were explained as "bad luck." Everybody hates that non-answer. I'm still looking for an answer.

I am a 26 year-old wheelchair user. I ended up paralyzed from the waist down after a tumor in my spine left me paralyzed around the age of 6. I was afraid that I was going to have a hard time getting pregnant because my periods were irregular and my hips were small. To my surprise, I got pregnant pretty easily after I started dating and having sex with a guy that was obsessed with getting me pregnant. I was in love with him and thought that he really did want a baby with me. My therapist later said that I had "Stockholm Syndrome." The father of my babies was a psychopath.

In 2017, on Saint Patrick's Day, I had my green socks on and we made a baby. I was thrilled, he was indifferent. The biggest shock of my life was when I went to my 17-week appointment and my baby boy was dead. I named him Elliot. He was little and stopped growing at 14 weeks. His father wanted to make another baby the same day that I got out of the hospital. It was a fetish for him; making babies and then leaving. He did it to other women and he did it to me. A year later, I was pregnant again. I was terrified and I knew that something was wrong because the baby was hardly moving on the 12th week ultrasound. They said that the baby was probably sleeping and that I needed to cough and drink orange juice to wake him or her up. It didn't work, but there was still a strong heartbeat. When I went in for my 20-week gender/anomaly scan, my baby was dead. I wasn't surprised, but it hurt. I named her Levi before I found out that she was actually a girl. The pathology report said that her placenta was pale and dysfunctional. It broke my heart to know that she wasn't getting enough nutrients because of the placenta. I felt like I wasn't feeding my child. She stopped growing at 18 weeks and was bigger than her brother Elliot.

My boyfriend never came to see me at the hospital. He hardly responded to my messages. He disappeared and only came back when I invited him over for a drink. I was hoping to have some closure and finally had the guts to let him go and date someone else. The last time I saw him, I asked him why he wanted to make babies with me. He smiled and said, "Because I want to have options if I ever need an organ transplant; I bet our babies had good organs" he whispered in my ear. He was sick. His sense of humor was funny until then. I had become a mother and nobody was going to talk about my babies like that. I never saw him again. I never wanted to have another baby with him. I learned to love myself after grieving and getting pep talks from my friends and therapist. I become stronger and cautious about getting pregnant again.

I got into a healthy relationship after Levi died. We took care of each other and had great communication.

The only problem was - he didn't want to have kids. After my two miscarriages, I was sure that I wanted to be a mother. He broke up with me, so I could be happy. I wasn't happy, but I tried to pursue my dream by dating again.

Unfortunately, after the break up I was diagnosed with cancer. Another tumor between my heart and spinal cord. Little do people know that chemotherapy can make men and women infertile. Right now, I am in the process of freezing my eggs before treatment. My desire to be a mother is so strong that I don't even want to do chemotherapy. I am scared of what this will mean for my health and dreams. I promised Elliot and Levi that I would give them a living brother or sister and I cannot let them down.

Feel free to reach me at #studyofthesoul on instagram or Desiree Rodriguez on Facebook. If you can relate to my story in anyway or you found a reason for your second trimester miscarriages, I would love to hear from you. Everybody is welcome.

Love,

Another warrior,

Desiree Rodriguez
2/29/20

I promised Elliot and Levi that I would give them a living brother or sister and I cannot let them down.

Erin

Dear Warrior,

First of all, you are not alone. There is a giant community of warriors, like you and me, and slowly but surely we are becoming more visible. The infertility journey can feel so isolating and make you feel all kinds of emotions.

Let me summarize some of the emotions and feelings I have about infertility, perhaps you've felt them too. I feel like I am constantly waiting — for appointments, my period, TWW, scan after scan. It has been time consuming for the aforementioned reasons. It has felt uncertain - will I ever get to bring a baby home? It has felt all encompassing, touching every decision in my life, even if not directly related to infertility. It is hard. I have felt jealous, sad, hopeful, lonely, lost, unworthy, emotional, embarrassed, and broken throughout this journey.

There is no rule book in infertility and every emotion that crops up along the journey is valid. Acknowledge it, process it, and fight on. Believe me when I say those negative thoughts that have crossed your mind have crossed mine too. At times I've felt like I wasn't infertile enough. I was able to get pregnant with IUI and haven't moved on to IVF so sometimes I felt like I didn't quite fit in with the infertility community. But I have realized, I do, just as much as anyone else. If you are enduring infertility there's no comparing your situation to anyone else's and it surely isn't a competition.

Although our stories are unique to us as is how we process and move forward with them, there is an intrinsic understanding of what we want and the sacrifices we are willing to endure to bring this dream of parenthood to fruition. I never thought I would be able to give myself an injection, but here I am doing it. I also never thought I would let my husband give me an injection, but there he is doing it.

With infertility and any pregnancy there is no guarantee. I teeter on two worlds, not realizing either really existed, no one around me experienced these things, no one talked about these things. In 2018, we began our journey to grow our family with a little help from science. We went through three medicated cycles, two IUIs, two pregnancies, and subsequently two early pregnancy losses. Then came our beautiful daughter, Lani, on our third IUI. I thought we were finally through it, we had overcome infertility. I wouldn't need to stick myself with another needle ever again. My pregnancy was full of hope but also so much worry from our first two losses and infertility that I just felt unsure the entire time. I didn't get to experience that blissful carefree pregnancy we see all over social media. My daughter was born severely premature at 23W5D. She lived for 20 minutes but ultimately was just too little to survive. My heart has been ripped out of my chest and crushed every day since she died. The grief I have for my daughter is real. The grief I have because of infertility is also real and has added an extra layer of grief and doubt on this journey to motherhood. When I found out we were pregnant, I felt like I worked so hard and finally all my sacrifice paid off. I feel like infertility in some ways robbed me of my naivety about pregnancy loss. But infertility made me so appreciative of the life growing inside me, thankful for each day and every symptom of pregnancy.

So here I am - an infertility warrior and a bereaved mother. A lot of women I have encountered who are in this infertility battle have also found themselves in the pregnancy and infant loss community as well. Although I don't ever want pregnancy or infant loss to be "normal," I want people to realize it exists and you are not alone! The women I've met on both these paths are some of the best ones I'll ever know.

This journey really feels like you're just surviving from one day to the next at times. I want you to know it's okay to say "no" to anything that is triggering, whether a baby shower, birthday party, or lunch with your fertile and/or pregnant friend. Mute, unfollow, block do whatever you need to do for your own emotional well-being.

I found that the more boundaries I created and the more open I was with my infertility the less complicated and stressful my life felt. I didn't need to make up excuses or worry that I'd look flakey to my friends when I cancelled plans at the last minute. I didn't need to hide my medications and silently sneak off to give myself an injection at events. I was just doing what I needed to do to grow my family, less strings attached, and putting myself first for a change. And I will continue to do whatever I need to do to preserve my own happiness.

Whatever decision you find yourself making through

everything, it is what is best for you, whether you feel guilty or feel selfish, you are not. You are doing what you need to do for your family!

The path to parenthood isn't always linear. You matter, your story matters. You are worthy of being a parent.

From an infertile (& bereaved) mother — YOU GOT THIS!

XO,

Erin

IG @eepsbobeeps

I found that the more boundaries I created and the more open I was with my infertility the less complicated and stressful my life felt. I didn't need to make up excuses or worry that I'd look flakey to my friends when I cancelled plans at the last minute. I didn't need to hide my medications and silently sneak off to give myself an injection at events. I was just doing what I needed to do to grow my family, less strings attached, and putting myself first for a change. And I will continue to do whatever I need to do to preserve my own happiness.

Katie

And so you walk away, the tears are stinging your eyes. You want to run to the car, but you have to try and act like everything is ok. Act natural. But for you, your natural is falling apart.

You hope no one is following behind you. You get to the car, fumble the keys and unlock the door and get in as quickly as you can. Turn the car on, barely do a head check and pull out quickly, the hot tears are now running down your cheeks and you wipe them away. You turn up the music, trying to gather yourself and not completely fall apart. And you do this every time there is another baby shower, a new baby to visit, another kids birthday, another family event, another time that you feel happy for someone else, but your own life is falling apart as you just cannot seem to fall pregnant. You cry as you feel that there is something wrong with you, your body has failed you, is failing you and it feels as though it is all your fault.

Why do babies come easily to some and not others?

My story began when I was diagnosed with breast cancer at 28. My husband and I had just got married and bought a house. We were starting our lives together and planning on starting a family when I was diagnosed. And what followed was a minefield of doctors, medical appointments, surgeries and procedures. But nothing could really prepare me for the emotional and psychological damage I was to endure. My cancer, and it's genetics, were what led us down the path of IVF in the first place. We tried to genetically test embryos for the BRCA1 gene in the first place, hoping to avoid passing the gene onto any future children, but unfortunately my fertility was far too compromised from my treatment and our brilliant fertility specialist deemed it would be hard for us to fall pregnant full stop, after our first failed cycle. I felt incredibly unprepared for this outcome, as in my head I just naively thought we would do 2 cycles of IVF - back to back - and have at least 6 viable, testable embryos and we would get our 2 children from them. I really should have known better with how medicalised my life had become since my diagnosis.

I was completely unprepared for the emotional toll that IVF would take on me. In tears every day. Unable to talk about it and the constant pain and hardship I felt from being in my situation. My age meant everyone around me was getting pregnant and I felt as though no one could truly understand how I felt. My cancer had not only taken away my breasts, my hair, my ability to breastfeed any potential children, my dignity in so many ways, but it had now taken away my ability to have children naturally, and potentially the only thing I had ever really wanted to be - a mother.

When I was finally pregnant with my daughter, my anxiety was through the roof. How could I keep this baby (who was so hard to conceive) safe for nine whole months? Once I could feel her move, every night I lay awake for hours, trying to make her move, as the stress of her not moving was huge. Once she was here, I couldn't quite believe I had a little girl. And I must say I think those first eleven months of her life were the happiest I have ever been.

I think there is a perception from the majority of people - who don't understand the IVF process – that you will do IVF and have a baby. I even think I really thought this. The trouble is, you just don't hear about all the stories where it does not work out for people. Maybe because it's too painful for them to talk about. It's often assumed they didn't want kids. But perhaps they tried for years and years and it just didn't happen for them. I also now understand the addictive nature of it. It's like gambling - just one more cycle. What if we just try one more time? Maybe that will work. When is it ever truly right to give up? How do you know the next time it won't work?

The thing is you will never know when the right time is. I can see how this destroys people. For me, I felt as though everything that made me a woman had failed me. I felt as though my body constantly failed me. I felt as though I was constantly letting down my partner - who has been my one constant through this all. I truly believe no one can understand this situation until they are in it. No one who simply had a baby naturally and easily can understand what it is like to be trying to conceive through IVF. They cannot understand the grief you feel at almost every circumstance in your life. And once you go through the IVF door, it is no longer "fun" to try and get pregnant.

Some people have commented to me that it must be so exciting to be doing IVF. Their assumption is you will get pregnant. They do not understand what you will put your body and mind through to try and conceive a child. They do not understand at the end of the day it is a gamble. For all the pressure you go through –

mental, physical, emotional and financial – it may not work. It is one of the rare things where you can actually end up worse off than you did at the beginning. And end with nothing, no embryos, no baby. Just your hope, trampled on that little bit more.

I stupidly thought that when we started trying for a second child I would be okay. My daughter was eleven months old and I just thought because I had her I would be okay. I had always promised myself I would not be that person who became totally caught up in having a second child, when I was lucky enough to have one.
But as soon as we started the IVF process, everything came flooding back and it was so much worse than I expected. It was different, but almost as bad as the first time. There was a pressure, from myself, to produce a sibling for my daughter and another child for my husband.

The feeling of being alone is very real with infertility. I always found it hard to remember there were people similar to me, going through the same things. Simply because IVF and infertility is not spoken about.

Feel angry, feel sad, feel excited, feel hopeful, feel betrayed - feel all the feels. And try to remember someone else feels this too. It may not help you in the moment, but it may make you feel that little bit less alone. I always have felt that I am not being negative - just realistic. And sometimes we need a good dose of realism in our lives.

Do you know what though? There is nothing wrong

with stopping. You are not giving up. You have done everything and there will come a point when you have exhausted the options, exhausted yourself. I've been so close to that point. And in that last moment, when for me it almost felt over, I felt the relief of falling pregnant with my second child. And despite an awful pregnancy and stressful birth and first few months of his life, I felt relief.

For me now, this part of my life is over. But I don't think I'll ever forget the pain it all caused. What I lost over it. Even now writing this in the wee hours of the morning, after feeding my babe and my other babe is fast asleep in her bed, I still have the hot tears rolling down my cheeks. Welled up in my eyes. The feeling will never leave me. It will get easier. But it will stay with me. And I think I am all the better for it. For my children are the most precious thing to me.

One thing's for sure - all this has been worth it. I can honestly say, my two children, they are the best things I have ever created. They are my everything.

Katie

For me, I felt as though everything that made me a woman had failed me. I felt as though my body constantly failed me. I felt as though I was constantly letting down my partner - who has been my one constant through this all. I truly believe no one can understand this situation until they are in it.

Angela

Title: Coping Through The Unexpected During a Pandemic.

Hi. My name is Angela. Since a very young age, I wanted to be a mom. As a child, I would pretend that I would be feeding my baby the bottle as I sang "you are my sunshine." When I met Paul in 2016, I knew he was the one. After years of being together, he proposed to me under a tree of Christmas lights and surprised me with a box of cannoli's. I was ready to not only spend the rest of my life with him, but to grow together as a family and live happily ever after. Weeks before my wedding day, I got the devastating news that I had Diminished Ovarian Reserve. I was in shock because I was only 28 years old. My doctor said, "You can still get pregnant but your clock is ticking a little louder than others."

After many cycles of Clomid and unsuccessful attempts to naturally get pregnant with Paul, my doctor recommend IVF. I was scared of IVF. IVF was our last resort. I researched all the stories from people all over the world. The countless shots, the financial burden and the emotional reality that IVF was not a guarantee that you would bring a baby home. I wasn't ready to take the IVF leap. After all, I was only 29. We proceeded with IUI.

My first round of IUI was not exactly a breeze. Instead of naturally having sex in the comfort of our own home, I had to rely on doctors to help my husband and I have a baby. The hormone drug Clomid caused crazy up and downs emotionally. One day, I was sad and the next angry. I didn't want Infertility to define me, but it did because everywhere I turned someone was pregnant. I was so happy for my friends and family members and I was sad that my body was continuing to disappoint me. Eventually, due to Clomid side effects, I felt like didn't even know who I was anymore. I had sleepless nights, nausea and migraines. Despite the side effects, I kept moving forward because I desperately wanted to be a mother.

After an entire year of fertility treatments, I finally got two lines and was pregnant from round 1 of IUI. My husband and I was so happy that we beat infertility. I instantly planned our future together. My beta numbers doubled but not as much as my doctor have wanted. I was still optimistic. When you find out you that you are pregnant, it is supposed to be the happiest day of your life. For me, every day I was on edge. Am I still pregnant? Every day I would get the call that my levels doubled but not in the way it should be. I quickly realized that I was on a horrible roller coaster that wouldn't stop. I went to the clinic every day for countless blood work until it was finally time to go in for an ultrasound. The nurse warned me that it could be an ectopic pregnancy.

 I remained positive by singing baby beluga every night to my tiny baby growing inside me. Then one day I went to the bathroom and noticed bright red spots. My doctor had me come in for an appointment sooner. I was determined that I wasn't going to lose this pregnancy. I held my breath as the doctor came into the ultrasound room. I will never forget that summer day of July. I saw the heartbeat flicker like a sparkle in the night sky. It took my breath away. I hung our very first sonogram on the refrigerator. When you see the heartbeat, your miscarriage percentage goes down.

Unfortunately, I was the unlucky one. My first sonogram was going to be the first and last memory of my baby. Late in the night, I woke up to heavy bleeding and excruciating labor pains. My cat comforted me by having her paw on my belly. I called my doctor. My doctor said "no matter what happens between now and the hours on, this pregnancy loss is not your fault." Tears rolled down my face as I thanked her and hung up the phone. I wasn't ready to let go of the pregnancy, but I had no control. 5 hours later, I had my first pregnancy loss. It began to thunder and heavy rain like you would watch in sad scenes in a movie. Only my sad scene wasn't in a movie, it was my reality. When I woke up from a restless night, I cried because I knew I was no longer pregnant and back in the club of infertility.

Slowly I picked up the pieces from my first miscarriage. People chimed in and said that I was still young and that I can try again. In fact, that I should try soon because I am more fertile now after I'd miscarried. My closest friends and family told me not to stress and that it will happen. I wanted to run away every time I heard those hurtful words.

We proceeded with our second round of IUI. To our surprise, our second round of IUI was successful. I was nervous that I would have another miscarriage. I tried to be optimistic and reminded myself that every pregnancy is different. I was grateful to wake up every day and still be pregnant. I had a high beta number. Then all of a sudden, I had sharp pain on my side. My beta levels dropped and I had to check for an ectopic pregnancy. As I went in the pregnancy unit hospital, I could hear babies crying and heartbeats on the doppler. I was in denial that this would be my second miscarriage. On Christmas Day, I told myself that this time next year I will be holding my rainbow baby.

Months passed by with no success. IVF was our only option. I was so sure that my first round of IVF would work. I was quickly surprised that my retrieval failed due to poor response. Paul and I had no embryos. I had to go through another road of shots, blood work, ultrasounds and being put under anesthesia for an egg retrieval. During our second retrieval, I was able to get 3 eggs. I anxiously waited 5 days to see if the embryos not only fertilized but kept on surviving. The wait of hearing how many embryos you still have brings a lot of anxiety because you are afraid to get bad news. I was so thankful that we had 3 embryos. It only takes one as what I hear a lot of people say in the IVF world. We did a 3-day fresh transfer of the highest grade embryo. It didn't cross my mind that my first transfer could possibly be unsuccessful. I was highly confident that this first embryo would be my rainbow baby. I sang baby beluga to my embryo picture every night.

When I found out that our first transfer failed, I was

angry and confused. How come I got pregnant twice with IUI but not with the highest graded embryo that I worked so hard to get for the past 3 months? I continued with my second transfer. I let go of all the doubt and fears from my past failed fertility treatments. I had hope that this IVF round would finally be my time. Two weeks later, I had another failed embryo transfer. I only had one embryo left. I felt defeated. I wanted my husband to throw away the sonograms of my embryos but quickly changed my mind. Even though those embryos hadn't survived, I felt like I suffered a miscarriage. A failed transfer and a miscarriage felt so similar to me. I felt so angry at the situation I was in with IVF. I felt like no one understood what this process is like.

I quickly realized that I couldn't control the outcome of IVF. My doctor told me that I had to try to be positive and to give the best chance with my last embryo. I went in with my last transfer as whatever will be, will be. I let go of the past even though it haunted me. I had PTSD and anxiety due to the many years of infertility. My last embryo transfer was amazing like the others. It felt like you were on cloud 9 and that you were so very close to being a mother. After all, you do all the shots, countless bloodwork and ultrasounds. When you get your picture of your embryo, it becomes oh so real and magical.

During the two week wait, I processed it differently. I felt at peace. Maybe this last embryo was the one. I didn't analyze my two week wait symptoms. I wanted to still feel like I was on cloud 9. My dog and cat were so in-tuned with my body and never left my side. I took a pregnancy test the day before my beta. It was finally positive. I was so relieved and scared. Will I have another miscarriage? I decided to treat each pregnancy as a new adventure.

I was so grateful to wake up every day and still be pregnant. I was incredibly nuaseous but I didn't care. Then, one morning I woke up and didn't feel sick. Even though I had no bleeding, I had a very bad feeling that something was off. When I went in for my first sonogram, my worst fear came true. There was no heartbeat. I was not only miscarrying but I had no remaining embryos of IVF. There are no words to describe how it feels when you have no remaining embryos from IVF.

Will I ever be a mom?

I had to go through an D & C and thought I was to be put under anesthesia. When I got hooked up to the IV at the clinic, I was informed that I actually was going to be awake and only slightly sedated.

The doctor said that I can be transferred somewhere else to be put under anesthesia. He told me that it would take days or weeks for an appointment. I have gone through enough pain and heartbreak, I didn't want to be sick from the pregnancy and be constantly reminded that my baby no longer had a heartbeat. I decided to move forward with the procedure. I wanted answers to why I keep on miscarrying.

The D & C experience was a nightmare that I never want to relive again. As I was lying awake and sedated, the doctor performed the procedure. The medicine took the physical pain away but not the emotional trauma from it all. As my baby was taken away for testing, a part of me was also taken away. I felt like a part of me had died. While in recovery, I was in excruciating pain that lasted for a long time. It felt like I was in labor. The pain got so bad that I had to go back to the procedure room to make sure everything in my uterus was cleared. The doctor told me that I had low pain tolerance and recommend for future pregnancies losses to be put under anesthesia. He apologized for the experience. I spent a few days in bed and shut off everything from the world. I had restless nights due to nightmares. A week after my D & C procedure, I switched fertility clinics in hopes for a better outcome. I didn't want to take more days off to grieve. The emotional pain was too much to handle. Pushing forward with fertility treatments was my way of coping and the only thing I could control.

Round 3 of IVF and more shots, blood work and ultrasounds came my way. When I woke up from egg retrieval, it was the first day it snowed and Christmas music had began. I had one egg that didn't have a fighting chance to survive. My new doctor told me that he was very concerned about my low amh. He gave me the harsh reality that round 4 of IVF would be my last round with him before recommending donor eggs.

It wasn't until Christmas Day that I finally had a break-down. I remember last year on Christmas Day, I told myself optimistically that this year, I would finally have a baby in my arms. However, here we were, still childless with lots of angel babies watching over us on Christmas Day. I used food for emotional comfort which resulted in a binge eating disorder. I was not ok. I had to seek professional help for not only my eating disorder but how to grieve all the losses that I have en-countered. I didn't realize so much pain that I pushed under the rug. I had to grieve the loss of not being able to get pregnant naturally. I had to grieved the loss of failed transfers, failed IVF treatments and pregnan-cy losses. All the losses built up over time and I didn't know how to handle it. I turned to food for comfort instead of seeking help. I felt like I was out of control. I eventually sought out a therapist and a nutritionist, needing to find myself again.

I was more ready than ever to start my fourth round of IVF. I had my fertility medicines and shots read to go. I was determined to start when the unexpected happen and I got a call from my clinic. My nurse told me that all fertility treatments are cancelled until further notice due to the pandemic of COVID-19. My nurse told me that all fertility treatments including IVF is considered an elective and nonessential. I was in total shock. I began to rationalize why fertility treatments should be considered essential. I became more and more bitter as I thought about it. How is it that my diagnosis of infertility is considered an elec-tive? Why is the desire of becoming a mom through fertility treatments is considered nonessential? What is the future going to look like going forward with fertility treatments once it resumed? I didn't choose to have infertility. Every opportunity matters, every moment matters when you have been trying to get pregnant for years. You fight even harder to want to become a mom when you see a heartbeat. It is perhaps my drive to keep pursuing IVF and not give up.

I was going to do whatever it takes to start IVF 4 during a pandemic. It was just going to get a little more complicated and more risks were involved. Risks of my husband not being able to come with in during egg retrieval and transfers. It was the risk that if I became pregnant, my husband might not even get to come to my monitoring appointments. Should I really proceed IVF during a pandemic?

I didn't want to do IVF, but it is my only option if we want to have a family biologically. At my age of 32 years old, you can say that I am young and that I have many years to start a family. That I should just calm down and relax. But the fact is that I actually don't have a lot of time due to my low amh diagnosis. My fertility clock is ticking.

After months of waiting, IVF round 4 began. I wore a mask to every appointment. I isolated myself and ate healthy. Before the egg procedure, I did the Covid 19 test and came back negative. I tried not to be too excited as I did the shots. But when they tell you have 7 follicles, you start to think that maybe this time of around will be different. I did stimulations for 10 days. On the last day of monitoring, my doctor told me I only had one big follicle. How could this be? She said the rest of the them couldn't catch up. My doctor told me I had to go through two options. I could go through an IUI cycle. My second option was go through egg retrieval with the possibility of having that one egg or none at all. I cried my way home and couldn't believe we are back with what with my last round of IVF.

I proceeded with an egg revival because I wanted to give it this best shot after all the work I had done. I couldn't sleep the night before the procedure. I prayed and prayed to let this round 4 be it until I was able to fall back to sleep. The morning of retrieval, I couldn't have my husband with me due to Covid 19 restrictions. I had to go alone. As I lay down and waited for the moment they call me in for egg collection, I became anxious about the outcome. I listened to Taylor Swift music and tried to zone everything out and focus on my breathing. When the moment came, I felt like I was going to explode. As the anesthesiologist put in the medication, I prayed one last time. I said out loud, "oh god I hope this works out" as I quickly fell asleep.

When I woke up from the procedure, my first words were "did you get the one egg?" The doctor said yes. I took a deep breath and was relieved. There was nothing I can do at this point. I just had to hope for the best. I waited anxiously the next morning. The one embryo had fertilized.

I hope that this embryo will be the baby that I can finally bring home, the baby that my husband and I have been fighting for.

Angela Rosano-Orlando

My closest friends and family told me not to stress and that it will happen.

I wanted to run away every time I heard those hurtful words.

Kirsten

To the Momma struggling to have her rainbow baby, I see you, sis.

To the Momma with PCOS who feels let down by her body, I see you too, baby girl.

I feel your pain and it hurts, doesn't it? Not only does it hurt, but it really fucking sucks.

I see the disappointment on your face and the tears in your eyes with every negative pregnancy test you take. You question why you would put yourself through that heartache again this month, but you can't help but think, 'this could be time I see those two pink lines.' You've been let down again.

You begin to blame yourself, shame yourself, and question what you're doing wrong, what's wrong with you. You try to hide the pain from your husband, bottling it up inside, not knowing that your mood tells him that something's wrong. You don't want to tell him because you don't want to say it, you don't want to let him down too, and you don't want him to see you crumble.

I see the hope in your eyes when you start a new month and a higher dose of fertility medication. I see your struggle with the infertility diagnosis. I know you're tired of going to the doctor. I understand your anger with your insurance company and that there is such a financial burden to have a child. I want to scream from the mountaintops with you that it just isn't fair.

I hear your prayers, your cries and promises to God. I hear the excitement in your voice when you talk baby names with your husband. I see you scrolling Pinterest for hours, designing the perfect nursery, and saving all of the must haves. I feel the tug at your heart strings when you walk by the baby section at Target and you just can't help but imagine the little one you long to hold in your arms in one of those sweet outfits. I see that hope go away in the blink of an eye when the realization sets in that you may never get that chance. I see the fear take over, your lip starting to quiver.

I hear you wish for something you never thought you would – your period. You just want your body to be normal for a couple of months so you can use your Flo app like all of your friends. You just want to spontaneously be intimate with your husband instead of making a calendar of the days you 'have' to be intimate. I feel your frustration because you feel like it's more of a chore than the love you know it truly is.

I feel your anxiety in finally deciding that you want your rainbow baby; the one you weren't sure you would ever want. I feel your anger that it took you so long to come to the decision to have another baby and now you can't. I know the what ifs that go through your mind every day. I hear you sob to your husband the fears of having to experience the loss of another child. I feel your hope that 'this time' you'll get to bring your baby home from the hospital. I see your hesitation is setting up another nursery. I feel the heaviness in your heart questioning that 'maybe it just isn't meant to be since it's not happening.'

I see you, sis.

Do me one favor, okay? Don't give up. Don't ever fucking give up.

Your infertility does not define you. Did you hear that? Your infertility is not you.

Don't let the Devil in. Don't let him sit on your shoulder and tell you that you're not meant to be a mother and that it's not in the cards for you. Don't let that fear override your faith. Don't let your anxiety drive your mind crazy. That's so easy to say, isn't it? It is, I know it is, but the negativity can't take over if we don't put it into motion first. If you're anything like me, you not being able to be in control is an issue all in itself, but you do have some. You have control how you play the hand you've been dealt. Do it with hope and positivity. Keep trucking along.

You can do it, girl. I'm not telling you that it will be easy and that there won't be days that you don't want to crawl into a hole and bawl your eyes out, eat comfort food, and wallow in self-pity. There will be those days and guess what? That's okay.

You're brave, you're strong, and you're courageous. But do you know what else you are? You are worthy – you are worthy of becoming a mother and having all of your dreams coming to life in a tiny little being that you will one day create. Envision that day. Can you imagine the love you will feel when you finally look down at that beautiful little girl and see her smile for the first time? Can you imagine the overwhelming joy you will feel when that handsome baby boy squeezes your finger? All of the pain, the fear, the bumps and pot holes will have all been worth it. One day you will tell them how badly you wanted them, how much you prayed for them, and how thankful you are that you didn't give up.

Hang in there, sis. You are not alone. I'm thinking about you and I hope that one day, you and I will be sitting on our front porches, finally rocking that sweet baby we've both longed for, and we remember how strong we are and how far we've come.

We've got this.

With love and positive vibes,

Kirsten

You're brave, you're strong, and you're courageous. But do you know what else you are? You are worthy – you are worthy of becoming a mother and having all of your dreams coming to life in a tiny little being that you will one day create.

Melinda

Dear Complete Friend,

Thank you for reading this letter. It is a huge and important step in processing this challenging path, and I am honored you are welcoming me into your heart.

Whether expected or unexpected, perhaps you are missing a part of yourself -- a part that society uses to define us as women. When we grew into our womanly bodies, we anticipated menstruation with a bit of trepidation and excitement. It is sanguineous admission into a club that for years defines bathroom conversation, emotional states, conception timelines, and political rights.

I unexpectedly lost my uterus in a desperate surgical attempt to save my life. The child growing within, named Oak, did not survive either. I was immediately thrust outside of the doors of the menstruation club and into a limbo coldly labeled uterine-factor infertility.

When someone loses a limb, or even a testicle, support groups and community leaders are available to guide them through the pain, grief, and possibility of a prosthetic. There is no prosthetic uterus. Uterine-factor infertility is too often met with an attitude of indifference for an "unnecessary" organ. Those seeking uterine transplant are subjected to uprooting their lives to enter multi-year academic studies, along with physically and spiritually-taxing extraordinary rounds of IVF. The graciously donated organ is only temporary, with a goal of a single successful pregnancy, after which, the organ is removed and discarded. If one becomes a select few in this process, they frequently need to conceal their identities and go through this arduous process alone, shielding themselves from harsh criticism for partaking in something "unnatural." I know this, because I seriously considered it.

Seeking some resolution to my grief, I flew across the country to participate in multiple interviews with research doctors. They stated the same information repeatedly, intending to assess readiness. My different identities reacted disparately to this information. The registered nurse part of me understood these procedures as risky at best; the scientist part of me wanted to change the world through its results; and the hopeful mama part of me, well you know what she wanted. Ultimately, the rollercoaster of physical, emotional, and lifestyle requirements of being enrolled in a study - once canceled and then reinstated - led me in a different direction.

I realized the answer isn't in replacement, rather it is in reinvention. I held a ritual of saying goodbye to my period. As a reference to a popular Judy Blume book, I called it the "Are you there God? Meet the new Melinda" ceremony. I lit candles and cried over a box of tampons. I read a goodbye letter. I allowed myself to cry when I saw a pregnant woman walk by or viewed a post referencing the uterus for women's political rights. I joined an infertility support group. In this group I learned that infertility has many diverse representations, yet the feelings of heartbreak and hope unite us. Having a uterus doesn't guarantee a successful pregnancy, or even a pregnancy at all. The waiting is so much more profound than our physical organs. I want you to know that you are not alone. I acknowledge the hidden pain you carry from the space inside. I know the ache that comes from discarding those items that for years supported you each month. I too rub my belly when phantom pregnancy feelings arise. Or possibly I cannot touch my belly at all because of the painful reminder. I see your beautiful scars that indicate you are a powerful warrior.

We have other sisters, too. You might not see us or notice us because our missing parts are inside, but we see you. We see you as complete in your body. We see beyond labels, physical milestones, or possible outcomes, and into your core being. A uterus does not define you as a woman, or a mother; really, no body part does. To define a woman in that way is to minimize her to a collection of cells. Women are whole entities of power, light, and love.

I hold space for you, complete being. May you find yourself reinvented as peaceful, sound, and hopeful - knowing that you are supported - in all the ways you feel on the inside or the outside.

Melinda Peterson

IG: @_melindapeterson

We have other sisters, too. You might not see us or notice us because our missing parts are inside, but we see you. We see you as complete in your body. We see beyond labels, physical milestones, or possible outcomes, and into your core being. A uterus does not define you as a woman, or a mother; really, no body part does. To define a woman in that way is to minimize her to a collection of cells. Women are whole entities of power, light, and love.

Shannon

To one of the strongest women in the world:

This isn't where you expected to be. Maybe you got a surprise pregnancy with your first, and you want another. Except now you're tracking every aspect of your body. You watch what you eat because there's an old wives' tale that certain food can make you not become pregnant. You don't let your husband use his laptop too much. You don't let him wear boxer briefs or anything restricting in case they're hurting your chances. You do yoga, reiki, acupuncture, and meditate to stay low stressed. But no matter how much you try to ground yourself, no matter how many times you go to your favorite spots in nature to decompress – you just feel like you're struggling.

That's okay! THIS IS FUCKING HARD. Secondary infertility is REAL. It is as real as any other diagnosis!

Personally, I know more than I wish I ever knew. IUI, IVF, RE, and FET just to name a few. For 7 years, I struggled to get pregnant. After about 1 year of trying, my doctor put me on Clomid, Letrozole, and Metformin – not all together, but at various times. After these did not work, she referred me to a reproductive endocrinology, where I received my intake and I am not sure of much beyond that. I was basically told that I was too fat. My BMI was too high. A few years later, I went back to the same clinic, and even though I was heavier than I was previously, they did not find any issues that would deter me from using IVF and being successful. Even at the SAME clinic, just being evaluated by a different doctor I was able to be seen without judgment, but a doctor MUCH thinner than the previous – ironic? Don't stop advocating for yourself just because you may feel weak.

Then, it took time. It was **lots** of insurance pre-approvals (thankfully, my insurance covers IVF), waiting on prescriptions, waiting on my cycle, and sending positive vibes to the universe that my ovulation day wouldn't fall on a holiday or a day where they couldn't transfer. It involved acupuncture, long distance reiki, drinking pomegranate juice to thicken lining, and doing intramuscular injections of progesterone prior to a positive pregnancy test to make things "even better."

There were many hiccups along the way, whether it was a HCG check on a day where there was no one scheduled in the clinic, or being in the waiting room after your miscarriage to see a couple walking out going "that's my bean, that's my bean." But, every last "pothole" that I thought for sure was going to take me out, didn't. I survived that – it doesn't seem possible.

The loneliness and heartache consumed so many of my days, I am sure it has consumed yours as well. The waiting game isn't really a game at all. It's more of a form of torture - at least that's what it feels like when you're there.

But then, maybe you get those lines – the ones on a test that you took even though you were told not to – that you should wait for the HCG blood draw, and you see those two lines. TWO LINES. IT WORKED. Put this into the universe, close your eyes and see those two lines – feel those two lines. Manifest the shit out of that. But the BIGGEST thing to remember is that THOSE TWO LINES DON'T DEFINE YOU. You are a bad ass whether you get those two lines or not. And those TWO lines don't need to be an actual pregnancy test, they can represent anything – anything at all, as long as it makes you happy – that can be your own version of two lines.

Sending love and dragonflies to the BAD ASS you are,

Ellie & Cam's Mama –

Shannon

That's okay! THIS IS FUCKING HARD. Secondary infertility is REAL. It is as real as any other diagnosis!

Stephanie

Dear Fellow Warrior in Arms,

We have never met, but we share many similar experiences.

We have never met, yet we are walking the same path.

I bet sometimes you feel so alone that it is tangible. That sometimes no one understands what you are going through or how you are feeling.

The idea of going to a baby shower, seeing a pregnant person or a new baby can be so extremely painful that it can cause you to break down into gasping, gut wrenching sobs on your knees. Yet others just think you are being selfish or over dramatic.

They don't understand that your identity is wrapped up in this journey. That every day a small bit of your soul is crushed and eradicated. That every day, it becomes a little bit harder to hold on to hope and dreams.

I do understand. I walk that path every day. I struggle to be brave, to be cheerful and to hope.

After several years of marriage my husband and I decided we were ready to start a family. We tried unsuccessfully for over a year before seeking help. In that year we lost 4 children, 2 boys and 2 girls. After numerous tests we found that we were "just unlucky." How can they use a label like that to my face? Unlucky? Do they realise how small and insignificant that makes me feel when I am drowning in grief?

They gave us hope. They said IVF would be a success. They said we would have embryos to spare to complete our family. We were so happy to know all our pain and grief would be eradicated with a rainbow baby.

While undergoing IVF treatment a new type of isolating and loneliness came over me. No one understood the endless cycle of hope and despair as each cycle started and failed. They couldn't see how I could be so focused and involved with a tiny embryo. They couldn't understand my total despair at seeing motherhood disappear each time the blood test came back negative.

I don't think there is a relatable pain to being told you are infertile. You don't get it unless you experience it. There are not enough words to describe that type of pain.

I am so glad you understand. That you can relate to me and how I feel. So many can't and refuse to try. I can't tell you how many friends I have lost. How much of myself I have lost. I can't tell you because I know you know. I don't have to tell you.

I'm sorry I can't offer any words of hope. My story doesn't have the traditional happy ending. I don't have any living children, and I am no longer trying for them. I don't even have my husband anymore. Our marriage couldn't take the strain.

Instead, I can offer another kind of hope. That life can be happy without children. It isn't the dream we grow up on, but it is an alternate reality. Despite my grief and my losses, I am happy. Not every day and not all day. But I am happy. I can bring hope to others in my situation. I can help shoulder their burden and in turn ease my own. I can honour my children through this life. I can leave them a legacy.

Next time I cry into my pillow, feeling alone and misunderstood, I will think of you and feel less alone. I hope the next time you cry and feel alone, you will think of me and feel less alone.

In fellowship,

A Fellow Warrior.

Instead, I can offer another kind of hope. That life can be happy without children. It isn't the dream we grow up on, but it is an alternate reality. Despite my grief and my losses, I am happy. Not every day and not all day. But I am happy.

Wendi

Dear Mom Who is Waiting on a Rainbow Baby,

Repeat this after me, "it is not my fault." Miscarriage is so HARD. It leaves not only a hole in your heart, but leaves you searching for answers to help you find closure. While looking for these answers, all that we tend to do is continually beat ourselves up.

Stop. Repeat after me, "it was not my fault." I, too, am an angel mom. There isn't a day that goes by that I don't think of my sweet son in heaven and what his little life would've been like on earth. There's a special little hole in my heart from the tragedy of losing him. I know you must be feeling the same way too. Healing takes time, but it starts with you giving yourself grace in that situation. It was not your fault. When you are ready, give it to God.

Now, as you find the courage to try for a baby again, fear might still be lurking around the corner. That's okay. It's normal to be scared or worried that it might happen again. Pray about it and find support in other moms who are walking this same path. It always helped me to find blogs about it. They offered much comfort and words that expressed how I was feeling when I couldn't quite put it into words myself. It will give you comfort and validation. You are not alone.

Each month you're on pins and needles to see if your menstrual cycle shows up. I know the wave of emotions that come with every month and what a letdown it is on the first day of your period each month. It's a dark reminder that the wait is still ongoing for a baby, but please don't lose hope. If you can cling to hope as small as a mustard seed or a grain of sand, it will carry you through. Find family, friends, or groups online that offer more hope than you have. That's what you need on those really tough days. You need someone who will reassure you that "Your miracle IS coming and that God has not forgotten about you."

Do not lose hope for your rainbow baby. I promise you this, yours is on the way. Cling to that tiny seed of hope, even on the toughest days. There have been many times that I have almost lost all hope too. Right when I found peace about my baby in heaven and the fact that we had tried for almost two years with no positive pregnancy test, a miracle happened. My rainbow baby finally arrived. I could credit acupuncture, living as healthy as I could, exercising frequently, and so many others things to this mind blowing miracle, but God is the one who should receive all the glory. Prayers, lots of them, from me, family, friends, and even people I didn't know are what brought this rainbow baby into existence.

My advice to you, mama, is to cling on to hope - every day and know that loss is never your fault. Move forward and pray fervently. Start dreaming and envisioning your rainbow baby. Miracles are REAL and yours is on the way.

Sincerely,

Wendi
Angel Mom & Rainbow Baby Mama too

Repeat this after me, "it is not my fault."

Anne

Dear Infertility Warrior,

As I write this, my first thoughts are, I wish you well.
I have been in the same storm as you. Not in the
same boat, as all infertility boats are as unique as our
thumbprints. Just as a cruise liner experiences a storm
differently to a sailing yacht, my experience of the
storm is different to yours. But I do know this storm
well and, for many years, it stopped me from living. I
existed, but looking back now, I was not alive. I want
you to know and believe you are not alone, you are
valuable and worthy of love, peace, contentment. I
want for you a journey that gives you strength and
hope for a life well lived, with or without children.

This is my story. My infertility journey started quite
by chance. A conversation with my GP about irregular
periods as I discussed a prescription for birth control highlighted that maybe at the age of 30 I should
consider not putting off trying for a child. This sent me
into a spin. I was not ready. I had only been married a
few months. I had recently migrated to a new country
and was seeking to re-establish my career. I was still
young, wasn't I? I was ambitious to climb the corporate ladder and wanted to be in a financial position to
have at least 5 years off work while I raised my children.

Anyway, off I went to a Gyn/Ob, who suggested we try
Clomid but did not "see the point" of getting my hus-

band tested as I was the "one with the problem" (i.e. blood tests revealed ovulation issues). 7 months later, no pregnancy. I decided to take some time off work, as the general advice was "relax and it will happen." The first casualty of my infertility journey was my career, taking time off was not looked on very well in the corporate world. After 6 months I went back to work, out of financial necessity, back at a starting level position yet again.

A few years later, at 35, still no pregnancy. Husband still refused to get checked, but I decided to start investigating an IVF journey with an amazingly kind and considerate Gyn/Ob who I still see today. Tests revealed male factor infertility with very small chances of a pregnancy. The shockwaves that hit me were indescribable. How was I going to sail this Tsunami?

I got pregnant on my first try with IVF but sadly lost the twins I was carrying, and over the next 12 years with breaks in between, another 17 healthy perfect embryos were created and lost. I never got a positive pregnancy test again after the twins. Second casualty of infertility – my faith. Why God why? Why me? Why are child abusers allowed to get pregnant and I am not?

In those 12 years, there was very little support from the church I attended or Christian friends. We were no longer invited to many events as everything seemed to centre around children and family. There were pitying glances and furtive conversations about sin and lack of faith. The 3rd casualty of my infertility – my community.

Finally, at 42, after yet another unsuccessful embryo transfer following the retrieval of 18 healthy eggs but only 9 viable sperm, the Gynae suggested donor sperm which was strongly vetoed by the husband. Emotionally exhausted, financially depleted, and wanting to stop living on this roller coaster of hope and despair, I decided to close the book on trying for a child.

Did I resent the last 12 years? You bet I did. Did I resent my husband? Yes. Did I consider having an affair just so could get pregnant? Yes (but I didn't). 4th casualty of infertility – my emotional wellbeing. I went from chirpy and outgoing to morose and withdrawn.

The decision to end the IVF journey now brought me back full circle – my career choices at 42 were limited. I had settled for lower level jobs and avoided climbing the corporate ladder to keep stress at a minimum while on the IVF roller coaster. How do I now apply for the high level management jobs without experience and how do I explain to recruiters why I had not actively pursued advancement in the last 12 years, but opted for stagnation as it looked on my resume? It's strange - if I had taken a few years off to focus on raising my children and was seeking a career comeback, the response from recruiters would have been quite different.

So what do I wish I had known in the waiting time? I wish I had known about living in the liminal space. About being alive instead of merely existing in the time in between in the world of when and if I get pregnant.

I wish I had known about and made more informed career choices. I wish I had known that it is possible to balance career with the IVF journey with the help of career coaches and IVF counsellors. That it was okay to accept a promotion, look for career advancement, travel for work. And it was okay to make a choice to tone down a career if that was what I needed to survive IVF. I was not a failure because I was not an executive. It is ok to work at a lower rung of the ladder. But it is important to make these choices without regret, remembering that in the future, they were choices made on the path of least regret for a future I wanted. I retrained at 50 and am now in a career I love and enjoy every single day.

I wish I had known the difference between spirituality and religion. I wish I had known that church people do not equal God; whatever He / She means to me. I wish I had known how to find a supportive church with people who would not have questioned my faith or insinuated that somehow infertility was caused by sin. I am not a theologian so I won't go any further into this area, as everyone needs to find their own journey of faith and acceptance. I however, am now on a spiritual path that gives me peace and contentment every day. And it started with the serenity prayer – to accept what I cannot change, and the words of the ancient Chinese philosopher Lao Tzu, "When I let go of what I am, I become what I might be." I let go of being a depressed, pitied infertile woman to become a contented thriving woman with unresolved infertility issues. Semantics? Maybe, but definitely a huge shift in mindset.

I wish I had known it was ok to let go of people who aren't supportive and find my own tribe. Judgement, pity, and unkindness do not belong in my life. For my own emotional wellbeing, I do not need such people in my sphere. I now have a group of wonderful supportive friends with and without children and grandchildren. We laugh, love, and enjoy all that community has to offer. I also found a few supportive loss and childless-not-by-choice communities in the real and cyber world where I get my support when grief and loss are retriggered.

Mostly I wish I had known that I and I alone am responsible for my emotional and mental wellbeing. I have the strength and wisdom to make choices and stand in my own integrity on the path of least regret. That I what I think of me is more important that what others think. And that it is possible to be alive and thrive in the liminal space of waiting.

I would like to leave you with a poem by Judy Brown which has helped me live in the liminal space and allows my fire of life to burn bright again.

Fire
What makes a fire burn is space between the logs, a breathing space.

Too much of a good thing, too many logs packed in too tight can douse the flames

almost as surely as a pail of water would.

So building fires, requires attention to the spaces in between,

as much as to the wood.

When we are able to build open spaces in the same way

we have learned to pile on the logs,

then we can come to see how it is fuel, and absence of the fuel together,

that make fire possible.

We only need to lay a log lightly from time to time.

A fire grows simply because the space is there,

with openings in which the flame that knows just how it wants to burn can find its way.

I hope you, my dear Infertility Warrior, can find ways to create the spaces you need to burn bright amidst the logs of your infertility journey. I wish you peace, love, joy, and contentment. Namaste.

(You can find the poem "Fire" in three of Judy Brown's <u>books</u>: *The Sea Accepts All Rivers, A Leader's Guide to Reflective Practice* and *The Art and Spirit of Leadership.*)

Anne

Mostly I wish I had known that I and I alone am responsible for my emotional and mental wellbeing. I have the strength and wisdom to make choices and stand in my own integrity on the path of least regret. That I what I think of me is more important that what others think. And that it is possible to be alive and thrive in the liminal space of waiting.

Shannon

When I was younger and I heard of others struggling with infertility, I remember thinking "If this happens to me and my body won't let me have kids I guess it is just meant to be and I'll. . .adopt/be a dog mom/fill in the blank here." One miscarriage and months of the one little blue line indicating not pregnant, I feel embarrassed for those thoughts. What I've learned is to never to try to estimate how I will feel until something actually happens to me.

"Meant to be" may have its place and time, but I don't think it has any place or time in the world of pregnancy/infant loss and infertility. We live in a broken world where bad things happen and none of it is "meant to be." It's just what people say when they feel uncomfortable with the world's brokenness and their inability to control the outcome of things.

I promise you this wasn't meant to be. . . and I promise you is that there is hope.

Let me be clear though, hope does not mean things will end with the baby you want and how you want it. . .but maybe it will! What I mean by hope is that even though it may feel like this infertility defines you right now, it doesn't have to. You are not alone, you are not an outlier, and this is natural. There is a whole group of us out there (including many you know personally, but may have no idea) who are right here with you.

Nothing is wrong with you. You will be/are/have been a good mother no matter what that looks like. In the waiting time, know this - there is a community of us who are ready to love you, to share this burden with you, and meet you wherever you are on your journey.

You weren't meant to experience this alone, come find us <3

Shannon La Mar

We live in a broken world where bad things happen and none of it is "meant to be." It's just what people say when they feel uncomfortable with the world's brokenness and their inability to control the outcome of things.

Stephanie

Dear Friend,

I know. A piece of yourself is gone. Even when your surface is calm, grief's undercurrents tear at you.

You see, I lost two babies last year. We conceived our first baby, Ruby, through ICI on the first try. Everything pointed to me being the picture of prenatal health. Until the ultrasound showed us Ruby's heart wasn't beating. I'd never been swept off my feet by such a tidal wave of grief and pain as when I elected to take medicine to complete the miscarriage at home. Blue came so quickly after Ruby that I thought we'd be able to sweep all that pain away, a fluke we didn't need to think about anymore. But we lost him even sooner. At thirty two, I had the first surgery of my life to remove the placental tissue that my body just couldn't get rid of on its own, no matter how much I bled.

I learned that some experiences of pregnancy loss are fairly universal. The most comforting thing was when a friend could say, with true sincerity, "I know." Sometimes I didn't need or want to hear more than that.

And yet they didn't know. Those friends, being straight, didn't know what it was like to scramble for purchase in stories like my own only to find article after article by and for straight people.

I know, friend. I know what it's like to flounder while others find pieces of wreckage to cling to. I searched the far corners of the internet for anything that could reflect my wife's and I's experiences back to ourselves.

I know, friend. I know that translating heteronorma-tive material to be relevant to you is exhausting at the best of times and damn near impossible now. Don't put yourself through it. We queer folks already know what it's like to feel broken without pregnancy loss added to the mix. Stories like your own are out there, but if you can't find them, write your own rather than try to see yourself in a straight person's.

But I also know, friend, that if you've come this far, you've had the courage to say, "I am whole. I am not broken." We made it through the mountain of fertility and pregnancy materials that pretend we don't exist without breaking. That resilience will keep you mov-ing when you're soul weary.

I know, friend, - and I hope you do too – that you can take whatever time you need to find stillness in the storm. When I learned to sit with my grief instead of run from it, it taught me so much about my own strength. I'll never again believe anyone who thinks I'm weak. That process takes time, and that's ok.

Know, friend, that you are loveable, loved, and whole. You're just waiting for the sun to come out.

With love and hope,

Stephanie

www.rubyfruitnola.com
@rubyfruitnola

I know, friend. I know that translating heteronormative material to be relevant to you is exhausting at the best of times and damn near impossible now. Don't put yourself through it. We queer folks already know what it's like to feel broken without pregnancy loss added to the mix. Stories like your own are out there, but if you can't find them, write your own rather than try to see yourself in a straight person's.

Jen and Paul

Jen

January 2011 was the month and year that would change my husband, Paul and I's lives forever - we were expecting our first child. The next few months passed quickly - we were buying the things that we would need and I was attending all of my appointments where baby was growing and was healthy. Then it all started to go wrong.

I went to work as usual one Wednesday and one of my work colleagues noticed that my hands and feet were swollen so I got sent home and made an appointment with my doctor. At this appointment I was told that my blood pressure was high and that they would come to the house on Saturday to recheck it. A Health Visitor came to the house on Saturday told me that my blood pressure was still high and the I needed to go to the hospital.

When at the hospital I was seen by a gynecologist who told my husband and I that I was pre-eclampsia and that our baby probably wouldn't survive the day. This is where our world shattered.

I was in hospital for three weeks and over the course of the three weeks I had bloods taken and my blood pressure taken daily. At the start of week three we were told that I was going to be induced; I was in labour for three days. On the third morning of being in labour, Paul and I heard the dreaded words that no parent wants to hear "I'm sorry but there is no heartbeat." Our daughter had passed away during labour. Our daughter passing away was the hardest thing, something that no parent should go through. After some time, we decided to try for a baby again. Unknown to us this is was when our infertility issues began.

I fell pregnant again but sadly had a miscarriage early within the pregnancy and had to go to the hospital for surgery to remove the foetus. After trying for a family again, I had another miscarriage and thought that the chances of us starting a family were slim to nil.

In between trying for a family, we began the adoption process, thinking that this was our only hope in becoming a family. This wasn't an easy thing to go through as the social work department digs into your background and relationship and look for cracks. We got to near the end of this process when for no reason or explanation we were told that we wouldn't make suitable parents and they stopped us for going any further. This, as you can imagine, left us feeling really angry.

So after everything that Paul and I have been through, nine years later we are now going down the IVF route. Not knowing a thing about IVF and how it works we didn't know what to expect or how the process works. Thankfully we reside in Scotland so we are entitled to funding and can receive three cycles of IVF. To start this process, we had to be placed on a waiting list and when we reached the top of the list we received a letter with our first appointment on it. It was at this appointment we met our consultant who would be taking us through our IVF process.

After we met with our consultant I thought I was pregnant and this lead me to call the Assisted Conception Unit and our consultant for advice. I spoke to my consultant who gave me advice and asked me to call back two days later so I did and at the end of that phone call she said that she would call me back on Friday. She did not call and my husband and I were left worrying all weekend about what was going on with me. When I called the ward on the Monday and finally spoke to her she said "oh I thought that you would have called me on Friday when I hadn't called you back." Hearing this left Paul and I angry as we shouldn't need to be the ones chasing the professionals for answers.

At this point I would like to stress that if you aren't happy with any professional that you see during this process, then please, speak to someone. All the staff on the ward that we go to are like family as we see them so much. It's a small group of staff that you see on a regular basis so it's important to raise any concerns that you may have through this process.

So, onto the medication side of it. When I started the first cycle of IVF I was taking a nasal spray called Suprecur (Buserelin) to suppress the hormones that control the ovaries, I had to take this four times a day for three weeks. I then had to go to an appointment to have an internal scan to check the lining of my womb to see how thin it is (oh how I always feel like I need the toilet when getting an internal scan done). We were then told "you need to take the spray for two more weeks." So off home we went and I continued to take the spray. We then went for a follow up scan at which my lining was thin enough but now I had to take medication to thicken it up (bring on the needles!). I had to inject myself once a day for a week then went back in for another scan (while on injections I was also taking the nasal spray). The injections were to help produce my follicles so that I would have a good number of eggs for retrieval. I then had to take one final injection before egg retrieval day to make sure that my eggs were mature enough.

Then it was egg retrieval day. We had to be at the hospital for 9am. A consultant spoke to my husband and I about the procedure as well as an anaesthetist as I was going to be sedated. During our wait to be taken to the surgery room one of the nurses came to take Paul to a room to produce a sperm sample. The anaesthetist made me fell less nervous and anxious about going for egg retrieval as she found a subject that we can both talk about - we were both huge fans Harry Potter. So as I was being wheeled into the surgery room, this is what we were talking about. Then I was sedated and can't remember a thing about what went on during the retrieval process or what I was talking about. Ladies, it's a good thing to always ask later about the conversations that went on. Apparently I was telling the anaesthetist about Potter World at Universal Studios in Florida as we were there the year before.

Once home I then had to start taking a course of pessaries to prepare the lining of my womb for embryo implantation. The day of the egg transfer we had to be at the hospital for 9am again. We were asked some questions and then were told that someone would come get us when ready. Just before I had to go to surgery I had to go to the toilet to empty my bladder but as I had to have a full bladder for this I had to make sure that I only emptied it a little (it wasn't easy just emptying it a little bit while still making sure my bladder was pretty full). I had my embryo implanted then it was a waiting game to see if I was pregnant or not.

We were sent home with a pregnancy test and I was told when to take it exactly. Unfortunately, things didn't work out and the first cycle didn't work for us. My husband and I started going through IVF just before COVID-19 struck and we were lucky to have gone through and completed cycle one before the hospital postponed all treatment.

Now we are in the middle of cycle two and, as I have a frozen embryo, the medication that I take is the same as cycle one but instead of injections I am on the nasal spray and tablets.

IVF is a long process and it's important to ask questions to the staff or let them know how you are feeling about things. The department that we are linked to has a counselling service, which my husband and I did make use of in the beginning and found these sessions very useful. It's also really important to always ask questions especially if looking for reassurance and if worried - just pick up the phone and call the team that are supporting you both.

Before we started our IVF journey, we went to New York for Christmas 2019 to have fun, make memories and get our heads around the fact that we were actually going down the route of IVF. Going through this process can put a strain on relationships so it's important to spend time together, have regular date nights and talk to each other.

Jen

Going through this process can put a strain on relation-ships so it's important to spend time together and have regular date nights and talk to each other.

Paul

As if the past upward struggle of trying to have a family with Jen and all our losses weren't hard enough; we were told we had to go through fertility treatment as our best option of having a baby.

So began another upward struggle - blood tests, lots of forms to complete and appointments with various people from our local hospital fertility clinic in Scotland.

It was established through these tests that we had what the doctors called "Unexplained Infertility."

All I could do was sit there and in my head think, "Oh no way, I was hoping that they would find something wrong and then that way they could maybe "fix" the problems."

Sadly, unexplained infertility was our diagnosis and we had to discuss with our doctor what route we would go down next. It was suggested that IVF was our best option. We discussed with the doctor how the treatment would work and we were sent home and advised they would be in touch.

We tried natural conception whilst waiting but again, no success. Then we got the letter that we were at the top of the list and that Jen was to start her treatment, which would be a combination of nasal spray and injections.

Jen and I discussed this but decided that we would start the treatment in the new year so we went to New

York for Christmas, which had always been a dream for us both. I guess that's also important when going through the treatment and that is to make sure you make time for just being a couple as the whole process can take its toll on you physically and mentally.

Then, in the new year, Jen started her treatment.

One day I received a letter saying I had to go in to produce a sperm sample....oh no!

So let's be real here, I had NO idea what to expect, but I initially was mortified at the idea of being taken to a room in a hospital away from my wife and left to just "get on with it!"

Nonetheless, that's exactly what was about to happen. I arrived at the hospital, but due to my hectic work schedule, I got the date wrong! So I was sent away and asked to come back a week later.

I went back (on the correct date this time!) and I sat anxiously in the clinic waiting room to hear "Paul Mills." I got up and was met by an attractive woman who was I would say the same age as me. So begins my blushing face, sweaty palms but still trying to act like I was cool and had this all under control. She led me down a small corridor to a door, opened it and oh dear there it was...a hospital grade easy chair. A quick scan of the room did not exactly "get me in the mood!" White walls, a sink and a hatch in the wall with lights and switches beside it.

The woman was actually very kind and explained

what I had to do with my sample and she also went through some paperwork with me, so I thought to myself that this was all very straightforward and my sense of embarrassment was now but almost gone. Then in leaving she said, "There are some adult magazines there if you would like to use them!" And BANG! I was back to blushing and sweaty palms!

I politely said thank you and locked the door once she left - guys this is very important to remember and lock the door if they aren't self-locking as anyone can walk in whilst you are "in the moment!"

I was there walking around the room and didn't want to touch the magazines so I thought I would use my phone…no WiFi or signal!

I then got to thinking, "Hold on, I have been in here for a while" Now, every guy is different I'm sure, but I was thinking to myself if I produce my sample to quickly than people think I'm too aroused to quickly but if I took too long then they might come in and check on me!

Needless to say I managed to produce my sample, left it in the hatch and swaggered out that room like I was an action star or the guy who conquered one of the 7 summits! (I have actually summited Mount Kilimanjaro which is number 4 but anyway I digress.) I felt good that I had contributed to our journey and I had to put into perspective that what I had to do was nothing compared to Jen - with her needles, tablets, vaginal medication and sometimes uncomfortable scans. My tests results came back as perfect sperm and then our treatment started but sadly we had a miscarriage.

At the time of writing this we are now on our second round of treatment using our frozen embryo. Our clinic said that they can freeze our embryos for 10,000 years; medical science blows my mind!

In closing, anyone going through fertility treatment - make sure you have a support system and do what feels right for you when it feels right for you. If you aren't happy with your clinic then tell them, ask as many questions as you want and please remember that no question is stupid. Believe me I asked plenty of questions! But above all try and smile even when you feel you can't take the stress anymore.

Paul

Anyone going through fertility treatment - make sure you have a support system and do what feels right for you when it feels right for you. If you aren't happy with your clinic then tell them, ask as many questions as you want and please remember that no question is stupid. Believe me I asked plenty of questions!

Katie

Five weeks after our wedding we had our first miscarriage. Here we were supposed to be in wedded bliss and instead we were grieving our first loss. As a labor and delivery nurse I knew that they happened "all the time." My doctor said that 1 in 4 women experience a miscarriage and go on to have a healthy pregnancy. I should be fine, they said.

4 months later I experienced our 2nd miscarriage. I had an early ultrasound at 6 weeks for spotting, we saw a heartbeat. Everything was growing as it should. The spotting continued very lightly till 7 ½ weeks. I went back for my normal 9-week appointment and here was no heartbeat, the embryo appeared to have stopped growing at 7 weeks. I was offered to wait out the miscarriage, take misoprostol or have a D&C. I choose to do the misoprostol. It ended up being a terrible experience.

After the 2nd miscarriage I was left feeling even more alone, sad, and angry. I became depressed, I felt like I cried all the time. They forgot to mention how horrible hormones can be after a miscarriage. Besides the roller coaster of emotions, there is the roller coaster of hormones which can do a number on your body. I went back for a follow-up and I saw a midwife that day who said maybe I should make an appointment at the local reproductive fertility clinic. She said usually they wait till you have three consecutive miscarriages, but she felt that it would be a good idea for me to go. I didn't want to wait for my third to happen, so I gave them a call.

When I had my first miscarriage I considered myself healthy. I was active, ate a balanced diet, worked out, played golf, and ran. My only health problem was my thyroid. I was diagnosed with Hashimotos when I was in college. At the time I remember my heart dropping when I read that women with Hashimotos had a higher incidence of miscarriages. It was always in the back of my mind that I may have a hard time conceiving. So when my first miscarriage happened I thought it could be caused by my thyroid. I wanted so bad for there to be a reason instead of the common "it just happens." It's so hard to hear someone say "it just happens" or "just unlucky." When you lose something that has been a part of you for either a couple days to 40 weeks, to hear those words leaves very little comfort. We tend to always blame ourselves and think about what we could have done differently.

So far I've had 7 miscarriages and as much as I try not too, I still blame myself and my body. Either I didn't eat right, I drank too much wine, I didn't exercise either enough or exercise the right way or I didn't take all the vitamins I should have been taking. With each miscarriage I would fall deeper into despair. I did acupuncture, all the teas and herbs, gluten free, dairy free. I would take 10 vitamins a day. I felt alone and scared. I felt I had no one to talk to or reach out to.

All I ever wanted was to be a mom and what if that wasn't going to happen or maybe I would be, but in a different way than planned. My husband tried to be as supportive as he could be, but he just couldn't relate. There was this giant hole in my heart and each miscarriage made the whole deeper and deeper.

After the 2nd miscarriage I made an appointment at the local REI. They ran every infertility test, checked my husband's sperm, and did an ultrasound. They found nothing wrong. So we tried again, this time we waited 6 months between the last hoping giving my body a rest would be the answer. We got pregnant again. When we went in for a 7-week ultrasound, there was a heartbeat but the embryo was measuring small and the heartbeat was slow. I went back a week later with no heartbeat, I started bleeding the next day.

Again REI said there was nothing they could see wrong but that could do IVF as maybe there is something happening on a genetic level. We could test the embryos before transfer. As much as I was willing to try anything, I wasn't ready for that yet. I wanted to understand why I could get pregnant so quickly but not carry to term. In my mind my something was wrong with MY body. I wanted answers, even though I was being told there may not be any. We tried again 5 months later and had our 4th miscarriage at 5 ½ weeks. My cousin referred me to her MD in another state. I went for a 2nd opinion. The MD wanted to do exploratory laparoscopy and hysteroscopy believing it could be endometriosis. I had the surgery, which resulted in mild endometriosis and a few polyps. The MD was straight forward and said "This is not causing your miscarriages, I think it may be time to consider IVF."

My whole life I wanted to be a mom. Even as a child I was always holding my babies. I dreamed of having 4 kids, and being a labor and delivery nurse. How ironic to be a labor and delivery nurse and go through the struggles of miscarriages and infertility. I've seen my share of unwanted pregnancies and babies born with no homes. We are told as teenagers not to have sex, you will get pregnant and have a child. No one talks about the struggles of infertility. Our society doesn't talk about miscarriages or losses. We sweep them under rugs and bury them. We are expected to pick up the pieces the next day, with no time for grieving and healing. I called out for one of my miscarriages and when I went to check my time card it was marked as unexcused. I was expected to go to my job as if it never happened.

I wasn't ready to do IVF yet so we tried again, and had our 5th loss right around my 32nd birthday. I spent the month after again researching the internet wanting answers. My coworker referred me to her brother in law who was an REI also out of state. I was hoping for answers but we left there making the decision it was time to try IVF. He explained more about the possible genetics that could be happening and why he was confident that IVF would work. He also said "this is not your fault." My husband kept repeating those words on our way home.

The 6th miscarriage happened when we were waiting to start IVF. I was waiting for my period but it never came. You always hear those stories of a pregnancy happening right before IVF or adoption. For a few days I had my hopes but then the bleeding started. I was done. I was done with all of it. I think it made me even more motivated to start IVF.

We did one round of IVF. We sent 10 embryos off for
PGS testing and 5 came back normal. So maybe that
was our answer. Something was happening genetically.
We did a frozen transfer with an autoimmune protocol
steroid, aspirin and heparin and it took. 39+4 weeks
later we had our beautiful baby boy Samuel.

The pregnancy was a blur. I look back and I know I
compartmentalized through most of it. I have two
pictures of myself while pregnant. I did what I felt I
needed to do and that was to hold everything I had
close to me. I never really got to enjoy my pregnancy
or celebrate it. My miscarriages left me with so much
fear and mistrust of my body. But my body did do it
and I have to remind myself daily that, even with all
the losses, it did give my miracle baby boy.

My 7th miscarriage, and possibly not my last, occurred
just a few months ago. The pregnancy happened
naturally. We had planned to do another transfer but
I got pregnant instead. I was extremely fearful but, as
each week we saw a heartbeat my fears lessoned. By
the 10th week my husband asked if he even needed to
go to the ultrasound as everything had looked good at
the others. I asked for him to go just to be safe (When
I was pregnant with Samuel I went weekly from 6-12
weeks). We went in and immediately I knew something was wrong. There was fluid around the baby.
The ultrasound tech said, "I am so sorry but there is no
heartbeat." All the emotions came flooding back. I just
started crying and felt like I couldn't stop.

The MD came in, she felt like something appeared
wrong with the baby due to all the fluid. Thinking it

was probably something genetic. We scheduled a D&C for the next few days. They did genetic testing on the embryo. My MD called me two weeks later and said "It was actually a normal embyro and it was a boy." It was a crushing feeling that was so familiar. I couldn't go down the rabbit hole again. Being able to hug my son through it was what got me through. We may only have one child and I'm okay with that.

Many of my friends are now going through miscarriages or infertility treatments. I try to be open with them as I don't want them to feel the loneliness that I felt when I was going through mine. Infertility and the road to motherhood can be long and draining. It changes you. I hope that the more we talk about infertility, the less people feel alone.

Katie

No one talks about the struggles of infertility. Our society doesn't talk about miscarriages or losses. We sweep them under rugs and bury them. We are expected to pick up the pieces the next day, with no time for grieving and healing. I called out for one of my miscarriages and when I went to check my time card it was marked as unexcused. I was expected to go to my job as if it never happened.

Nancy

Dear Friend in Loss,

I get it.

Whatever it is you're feeling right now, I get it. And I know that other people – kind people, well-meaning people who love you – say the same thing. "I had a miscarriage between my second and third kids and it was awful. I get it!" No, they don't. They don't get it. But I do.

I understand that no one wishes you happy Mother's Day when you've had seven miscarriages. Because those babies don't count, apparently.

I understand that people are confused about why you could be so upset over losing something you never really had in the first place.

I understand what it's like to see pregnant women *everywhere*.

I understand what it's like to grow distant and separate from your friends who are having kid after kid after kid while you just want one.

I understand what it's like to operate in the world, meeting colleagues and strangers who have no clue what's going on with you, and wanting to scream, "I'm hurting! I'm grieving! I'm not OK but I have to pretend like I am because what other choice do I have?"

I really do understand all of it. And I hope that's at least some comfort - knowing that there really are people in the world who understand you.

But aside from that, I don't know what will help you get through this. It's been six years since my first miscarriage and I still don't know if I'm over the pain of that first one and the six that followed it. I imagine those seven babies in heaven, growing up without me. I imagine that they're being raised and loved by women who died in childbirth.

Is that being over it? I'm not sure.

But I can tell you what I did to help ease the pain. It might not work for you, but it did for me. For me, *doing* things and *creating* things helped. It didn't solve the problem, no. It just helped.

I took a painting class. I started beekeeping. I made lotions and soaps to give as gifts. I grew vegetables and flowers. I painted the house. Looking back, I now realize I did these things because I wanted things I had created, things I had made – things to look at and be proud of. Since my uterus wouldn't do it, my hands had to.

It kept me busy. It kept me sane. It gave me things to focus on, other than my misery.

And I guess it made me more interesting (and not in a "her-life-is-so-tragic-look-at-how-*interesting*-she-is!" kind of way). Interesting in the sense that by working to get through the pain in whatever way I could, I made sure my identity was more than just loss after loss after loss after loss after loss after loss after loss.

If that approach sounds awful, don't do it. Don't do any of it. You're reading this book, so you're already doing something, and since you're reading this book you know that there are many more of us – The Infertile – who get it. We understand you.

I don't know if my approach will help you, but I believe you'll have a happy ending. Maybe that happy ending won't look exactly like you thought, but you'll get there.

Thanks to my infertility support group, I know a lot of women with fertility problems. For a few, their happy ending was through IVF. For one, her happy ending was having an egg donor and giving birth to her son. For others, their happy ending was making peace with life without kids. Mine was through an egg donor and a surrogate – an amazing woman who gave birth to my son and to whom I am forever grateful.

Your happy ending is waiting out there for you. I know you'll get it. In the meantime, take comfort in the fact that other people get you.

Yours in loss,

Nancy Henke

I took a painting class. I started beekeeping. I made lotions and soaps to give as gifts. I grew vegetables and flowers. I painted the house. Looking back, I now realize I did these things because I wanted things I had created, things I had made – things to look at and be proud of. Since my uterus wouldn't do it, my hands had to.

Darcie

Brave Fertility Warrior,

I'm sorry this is so hard. This thing that seems *so* easy for everyone else. This thing that happens by mistake, with no planning or intervention, no pills or needles, no muss no fuss, no heartache.

It's not fair.

But it's not just one "thing" either, is it? Getting pregnant isn't just trying to conceive - it's your hope, your dream, the way you envision your family - your life. It's your baby and your parenthood. The fact that it isn't easy can very quickly get wrapped-up in your self-worth. Then you can find yourself spiraling into over self-analysis. That vicious cycle - the "yes, this is it - I feel different - I know this HAS to be it," to the letdown, the disappointment, the heartbreak, the grief. Then the self doubt can seep-in. The "I don't know what's going on with my body, or my partner's body, this will never happen." *None* of this helps. Then add in all of the platitudes that well-meaning people seem to never run out of - "just relax," "it will happen," "if you weren't so stressed about it all, you'd already have a baby." And don't get me started on the clueless, innocent questions that are so much salt in the wounds of infertility...the hurtful list goes on and on. But I don't have to tell you that - you know - and I see you.

I see you giving yourself the pep-talk every cycle, trying to invest your heart in it every single time.

It's exhausting and daunting and tortuous.

For me, my journey to parenthood started as someone I would eventually resent - we got pregnant in the first month of trying after getting off the pill. Honestly, we weren't even trying, we just stopped preventing. I assumed infertility was something I would never have to face, and while I was aware of it as a concept, I was just grateful that I didn't have to endure knowing more. Then at the end of our first pregnancy, just past our due date at 40.5 weeks, we got the devastating news at a routine ultrasound that our precious baby was no longer alive. She had a strong heartbeat at our appointment on Tuesday and by Thursday morning, she had died. Inside of me. I delivered her that night, though we didn't yet know she was a girl. We wanted to be surprised. After 4 hours of active pushing I gave birth to our first child. The first thing I said was, "Well, is it a boy or a girl?" "Girl." The doctor said it so quietly. It was all so heartbreakingly quiet. A girl. I looked at my husband and we knew her name was Mathilda - our powerful battler. I could write a book about my experiences around Tillie and what kind of Mother she has made me - but I will save that for another time. Another book perhaps.

After Tillie died we knew we wanted to try again. We were in those early stages of intense grief, and while it was suggested to wait a bit longer for our emotional well-being, we couldn't - we had to try as soon as it was physically possible. Looking back, I am glad we did. After months of trying, timing, and tracking ovulation with no success, we started infertility testing. Ultimately I was diagnosed with a low ovarian reserve. I was running out of eggs faster than I "should" have been at my age. So, while it didn't mean we *couldn't* get pregnant, it did mean that we had no time to waste and that we would need help. Not the worst news, but coupled with our grief it felt appropriately unfair.

So the plan was to try a few rounds of IUI and if that didn't take we would have to talk about IVF. After taking Clomid, going to acupuncture, internal ultrasounds to measure follicles, and a shot of Ovidrel to get the party started, we went in for our first round of IUI. It just so happened to be the day before Mathilda's first birthday. To say we were emotional wrecks is an understatement.

Luckily, we also decided to rescue our sweet pup, Zuzu the same day. We named her Zuzu after the youngest daughter in *It's a Wonderful Life*. Zuzu's flower petals are George's final reminder that life is worth living - and we certainly needed that reminder then. We were just trying to hold on to anything we could. Not to mention, holding on to any kind of hope was exactingly complicated because this thing that we so desperately wanted was a thing we were equally terrified of, because of our loss. The fear and the what-ifs were overwhelming.

I am grateful that we conceived on that first round. It was a gift to only have to endure one round, after all the testing and trying. All of the time spent trying for a living child was no small feat and it is something other people - who have not experienced the devastating challenges and losses we have - simply cannot even begin to understand. We held Tillie in our arms, we know her smell, her weight, her sweet skin. We had a beautiful child, and it is not fair to have to start all over again when all we wanted was her.

After the long-haul of pregnancy after loss, filled with more tests than I can count, we delivered our second daughter, Winslow - alive. Then, when she was eight days old, I knew something wasn't right. We brought her to the pediatrician who immediately called an ambulance to rush her to the ER. She wasn't getting blood to the lower half of her body, she had gone into shock, and she needed emergency open heart surgery. We were transported to Boston Children's Hospital where they saved her life, along with ours.

I have contemplated - if Tillie had lived, would Winnie have died? Honestly, if we hadn't experienced Till's death, I don't think we would have been as hyper-vigilant. We just knew from personal experience that terrible things happen and it doesn't always go to plan. Winnie didn't get an in-utero diagnosis - I just had a pit in my stomach that she was going to die. If I hadn't known that life is cruel, and babies die, and infertility is traumatic, I wonder if she would have had the more common outcome for her condition - she wouldn't have woken up.

I say all of this just to express that you will never be the same because of this journey. You will be a different person now. You will live in a different way than you ever would have if you weren't facing this. The grief and struggle of infertility and loss wear on you - emotionally and physically. I look in the mirror and can see it in my eyes and on my face. I carry it - like my love for Mathilda, like my fight for Winslow. Those experiences won't go away - they are a part of who I am, a by-product of the irrevocable change in me from navigating this path.

After all of that, we still knew that we wanted a living sibling for Winnie. I figured it would be a similar experience and we should get going as soon as possible. We started by testing my levels. Come to find out my AMH had dropped again, by more than 50%, and the red alert light in my mind started flashing. I stopped pumping for Winnie and got on Clomid to begin the IUI process again. It didn't work. I upped my Clomid - it didn't work. The two week wait became agony. I started dreading the emotional disappointment each cycle. I began to feel desperate and hopeless. It was scary and sad. I just had to keep trying and hope that my body could do it again. It was all so intense and after five unsuccessful rounds we were feeling incredibly defeated. We had one last chance. IVF would have been the next step, but we couldn't afford it. This was all we had left. The timing worked out that we would go in for our sixth and final round of IUI on the morning of my 37th birthday - that had to be good luck, right?! It worked for Tillie's birthday, so why not mine?

I went through all of the usual emotions in that two-week wait, all of the over self-analysis, the ups and downs - and it ended in two little pink lines. I took an extra pregnancy test to be sure - just like we did the first time with Tillie. We were pregnant again. We did it. Deep breath. Could this be my *boring* baby? The one who is born alive and can stay alive without a major surgery? Yes, and his name is Hugo. As I write this he is a sweet koala of a baby who is ten months old and gives hugs like he knows what we've been through.

I decided to get an IUD put in as soon as I could - the end of an era. I just knew we were done. It was sad - both me and my OB cried - we have been through so much together; we are forever linked. She is a true Hero of Compassion and I will love her always.

I don't know how your journey will end - what your family will look like when this era is over for you, but I do know that the struggle and the fight will be worth it because you will be able to look back and know that you did what you could - what was right for you. I can't guarantee it will be what you hoped for or dreamed of - but it will have made you who you are - a fertility warrior.

In love and solidarity,

Darcie
Mama to Mathilda, Winslow & Hugo

https://lostlullabies.weebly.com/
https://www.facebook.com/lostlullabies

I say all of this just to express that you will never be the same because of this journey. You will be a different person now. You will live in a different way than you ever would have if you weren't facing this. The grief and struggle of infertility and loss wear on you - emotionally and physically.

Waiting Time

In the quiet
That liminal in between
Rests a tiny seed

It waits
Like the pause between
The tick of a clock
Waits
Like the inhale of a breath

Watered by tears
Scattered upon the ground
Of the unruly unknown

It is warmed
By the sparks
Born of a persistence
Flickering
A calling to home

Until at last
In the long waiting
There is an exhale

It stirs
This tiny seed resting
Unfurling as the clock
Ticks
A threshold crossed

At long last
Life begins anew
Born of tenacious hope

www.ingramcontent.com/pod-product-compliance
Lightning Source LLC
Chambersburg PA
CBHW050733030426
42336CB00012B/1549